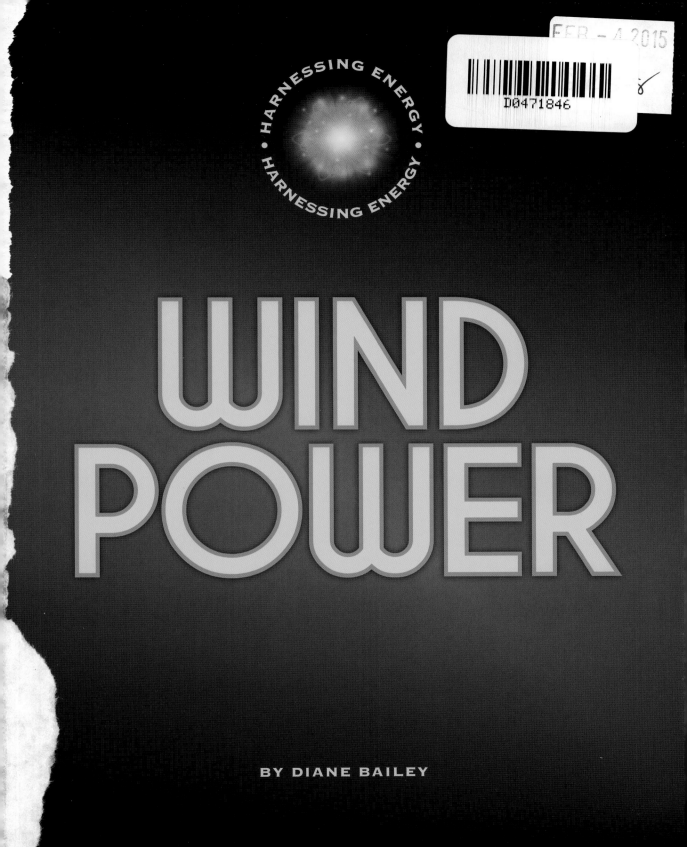

HARNESSING ENERGY · HARNESSING ENERGY ·

WIND POWER

BY DIANE BAILEY

CREATIVE
PAPER BACKS

TABLE OF CONTENTS

PEACE AND WAR. WEALTH AND POVERTY. PROGRESS AND SETBACKS. HISTORY HAS BROUGHT HUGE SWINGS IN THE HUMAN CONDITION, AND WITH EVERY CHOICE PEOPLE MAKE, THERE IS THE POTENTIAL TO MOVE FORWARD OR STEP BACKWARD. AT THE CORE OF THIS CONTINUAL STRUGGLE HAS BEEN THE QUEST FOR ENERGY. ENERGY GAVE HUMANS POWER AND MOTIVATED THEM TO DO GREAT THINGS—WITH BOTH POSITIVE AND NEGATIVE EFFECTS. WITHOUT ENERGY, PEOPLE WOULD NOT BE ABLE TO DRIVE CARS, OPERATE COMPUTERS, OR POWER FACTORIES. WARS ARE FOUGHT TRYING TO DOMINATE SOURCES OF ENERGY. FORTUNES ARE MADE AND LOST DEPENDING ON HOW THAT ENERGY IS MANAGED. THE LAWS OF PHYSICS STATE THAT ENERGY CANNOT BE CREATED OR DESTROYED. THAT IS TRUE, BUT ENERGY CAN BE HARNESSED AND DIRECTED. IT CAN BE WASTED, OR IT CAN BE COAXED INTO EFFICIENCY. CIVILIZATIONS AND TECHNOLOGIES HAVE LEAPED FORWARD—AND SOMETIMES BACKWARD—AS HUMANS HAVE TAPPED INTO EARTH'S SOURCES OF ENERGY.

Wind power is one of the world's fastest-growing energy sources.

In **medieval** times, when storms blew down dead branches from trees, peasants were sometimes allowed to take this wood for free and use it to warm their homes. This "windfall" was a welcome bonus in their difficult lives. Today, wind provides another bonus to people in the form of energy. Wind power has been used for centuries, but in the last 50 years, it's become an industry. On land and across the sea, from the Great Plains of the United States to the seas in northern Europe, wind provides electricity to millions of people. **Fossil fuels** are becoming scarcer, more expensive, and more problematic, making **renewable** energy much more popular. As people turn toward new ways of producing energy, wind power has a window of opportunity.

CHAPTER ONE

CATCHING THE WIND

FRIEND OR FOE? Ask someone that question about the wind, and the answer will likely depend on the conditions. Wind can be a cooling breeze on a hot day. Or it can come with gale force, as a tornado or hurricane that destroys homes and whole cities. Sometimes it's helpful, carrying seeds through the air to be **pollinated**. Other times it blows with such strength that it can remove an entire layer of soil that farmers need for crops. Wind is invisible and uncontrollable. But it's everywhere. And it doesn't cost a thing! The wind is full of power, if people can only catch it.

Most seed-producing plants and crops around the world rely on anemophily, or wind pollination.

As shown on this Polish stamp, ancient Greek ships used both oars and wind power to sail.

Ancient Egyptians, Greeks, and Romans used wind for transportation. The wind currents over the seas filled the sails of boats. On land, people harnessed the wind for other jobs. Early windmills provided power for tasks that were tiresome for people to do by hand, such as grinding grain or pumping water. Windmills were at work in Persia (present-day Iran) by about the seventh century A.D. The machines then spread east to Asia and north to Europe. The four-pointed Dutch windmill is a famous image. These brightly painted windmills served as landmarks and gathering places. They needed to be tended all the time, so sometimes people even lived inside them. Historians believe that, between the 14th and 19th centuries, wind provided about 25 percent of Europe's energy needs.

Wind energy powered much of Europe before the **Industrial Revolution**, but it didn't take off in the Americas for a long time. In 1883, a writer for the magazine *Scientific American* noted, "It seems incomprehensible that such a ready and potent agent [the wind] should escape practical use so completely as it does." That lack of use was about to change. By the turn of the century, farmers all over the U.S. were installing windmills that pumped water for cattle. However, wind never became a large source of energy, like coal or oil. In 1936, the U.S. government instituted the Rural Electrification Act to bring electricity to people who lived farther away from cities. The effort relied on fossil fuels, effectively putting smaller wind companies out of business. In fact, to get on the new **power grid**, farmers were required to stop using wind!

Wind energy made a comeback in the 1970s. In 1973, oil suppliers in the Middle East hiked up their prices, causing shortages everywhere. Nations started scrambling to find new sources of energy. One candidate was nuclear power, but it was risky and controversial. Henrik Stiesdal, a pioneer in developing wind technology in Denmark, returned home from traveling in 1976 to find that anti-nuclear activists had banded together to build a homemade wind **turbine**. He remembers, "For me it was a very big inspiration; I thought, 'Well, we can do it. If we want it enough, we can do it.'"

The U.S. also made a push for wind power. Because developing wind power sources cost more money than it made, businesses were encouraged with tax credits to pursue the technology. The early 1980s saw a "wind rush" in California. Instead of just a few windmills installed on family farms,

Windmills have historically provided energy to farmers and other rural residents.

With growing public awareness of fossil fuel pollution, people are looking to the skies for renewable options.

"wind farms" consisting of hundreds of giant turbines were sprawled across great distances. Several projects were built from 1981 to 1985. However, the boom was short-lived. In 1985, the tax credits expired. The wind didn't die down, but the industry did. This brief experiment had not lasted long enough to work out all the kinks. Many wind turbines were poorly built and broke easily. In addition, the oil crisis had passed by then, and prices came back down. Renewable energy didn't seem as important.

By the 1990s, the tide had shifted again.

The cost of oil and natural gas started to creep up, and many more scientists began to realize that fossil fuels were causing a lot of environmental problems. Emissions polluted the air and contributed to **global warming**. It was time to give wind another chance.

Wind power is distinct from solar power, but they are related. Today, the term "solar power" refers to energy that is captured directly from the sun. Wind power, though, comes indirectly from the sun. First, the sun heats the air. That warm air rises, and cooler air flows into the space underneath. The movement of the air is what we call wind. Approximately 1 to 2 percent of the energy delivered by the sun is converted into wind energy.

Energy comes in two forms: Potential energy is the amount of stored energy that can be used. A log of wood or a lump of coal has potential energy that is released as heat when it burns. Another form of energy is kinetic. This is energy that is released when something moves. A person running or an apple falling from a tree is demonstrating kinetic energy. Wind power works by harnessing the kinetic energy of blowing wind.

The basic principle behind wind power is that it is pure, mechanical motion. In the past, wind power was used to directly operate machines to do work. Today, there is an extra step. Wind is used to power a generator that makes electricity. In this process, wind turns the blades of a turbine. The turbine then spins a magnet in a generator that produces electricity. Of course, wind isn't available for pickup whenever people want it. Instead, capturing wind power is more like setting a trap. Most of the time, the turbines in a wind farm don't operate at their full capacity, because the wind isn't that strong. But when the wind does blow, the turbines are ready to grab it.

Lick your finger, and stick it up in the air. That's the old-fashioned way of finding out the direction the wind is blowing. Today, it's gotten more sophisticated. An **anemometer** measures the wind's speed and direction. Wind turbines typically operate when the wind is between 8 miles (13 km) per hour and 65 miles (105 km) per hour. Any slower, and there's not enough power to turn the turbines.

Forms of anemometers include handheld digital devices.

Higher altitudes mean higher wind speeds, making mountains good locations for wind farms.

Any faster, and the turbines can break. Sensors in the blades automatically adjust the pitch, or position, of the blades to receive the most power. Historically, it was simple to pick a site for a wind farm. When engineers saw stands of trees or bushes bent permanently to the side, they knew they'd found a spot where the wind was strong and steady. Today, they collect information about elevation, **topography**, and ground cover, and use computer programs to identify good places.

Over the last 100 years, wind technology has improved dramatically. Turbines have become more efficient and able to convert more of the wind that hits them into actual power. Just as the "how" of capturing wind energy has improved, so have the "where" and

"when." Faster wind speeds result in increased power. Double the speed of the wind, and the amount of energy it produces is eight times as much. Because faster winds occur at higher altitudes, turbines have gotten taller. There have also been developments in forecasting the wind. Wind may seem unpredictable, but it does have patterns. Today, scientists can predict the wind several hours in advance. That may not seem like long, but any advance notice is important when it comes to estimating how much electricity the wind can generate and helping to manage the power grid. Some areas are windier than others, but every country has at least a little wind. That's making wind energy an important source of power all around the world.

CHAPTER TWO

A BALANCING ACT

STAND IN THE MIDDLE OF A WIND FARM, AND IT'S LIKE BEING IN A SPRAWLING METAL FOREST. In many ways, a wind turbine is like a tree. The tower is the strongest part, like a trunk, and stretches 200 feet (61 m) or higher into the sky. The blades are designed to move, so they are lighter and more flexible, like the upper branches of a tree. The central piece of a turbine is called the nacelle. It seems small when looking up at it from the ground, but that's because it's so far way. In reality, it's as long as a

Although wind farms may span many miles, land between the turbines can still be used for agriculture and grazing.

A turbine's nacelle houses important parts such as the generator.

In 2008, France commissioned the Chemin d'Ablis wind farm.

The Dutch province of Flevoland installed more than 600 wind turbines as part of its energy initiative.

school bus. The blades can be 100 feet (30 m) or longer. They seem to swoosh slowly through the air, but that's also deceptive. In fact, the tips of the blades can travel faster than 200 miles (322 km) per hour at full speed.

Wherever there is wind, there can be wind power. About 80 countries the world over have installed some wind power generators. Add it all up, and wind makes enough electricity to power the homes of approximately 380 million people. In 2010, the U.S. and China were the world's top producers of wind energy. Together, the two countries generated almost half of the world's total wind power. The top five wind producers—the U.S., China, Germany, Spain,

and India—accounted for almost 75 percent of global wind power production.

While large countries such as the U.S., China, and India have the most wind power, they can thank Europe for jumpstarting the technology to produce it. Denmark, in particular, has pioneered wind technology, and for the last 50 years, it has led the way as Europe has developed the most established wind industry in the world. Many European countries have pledged to increase their wind power in the years leading up to 2020. A national government's attitude is critical to wind energy development—perhaps even more important than the wind itself! For example, Germany is not especially windy, yet it has a

thriving wind industry. By contrast, in Argentina, Russia, and South Africa, there is plenty of wind but not that much wind power.

Wind energy is popular in part because it does not pollute the air. Fossil fuel plants spew millions of tons of carbon dioxide and other **greenhouse gases** into the air each year. Wind farms don't put out any. As a bonus, the "fuel" is free. Historically, wind costs more than other forms of energy, but many people believe it's worth it. In the U.S., many large companies such as Wal-Mart, Starbucks, and Coca-Cola have decided to use environmentally friendly wind power for some of their electricity needs. An employee of the grocery store chain Whole Foods said, "The decision ... was made on the basis of 'It's the right thing to do' rather than 'What would the [financial] return be?'"

However, wind does have its drawbacks. Birds, bats, and marine animals (for offshore wind farms) can be killed by the spinning blades of the turbines. Large wind farms can disrupt habitats. The noise and movement also disturbs some people, even to the point of making them sick. Some people complain that large wind farms destroy the natural view of the land. Turbines may also interfere with how radio and TV waves are transmitted through the air.

The wind industry is no longer in its infancy, but it's not grown-up, either. Many people still think of it as an alternative form of energy that can't compete with the big boys of fossil fuels or nuclear power. One problem with wind is its location. People don't like to be blown around, so they tend to live in places that are less windy. However, it's impossible to put a batch of wind in a car and drive it to where it's needed. Since the wind can't be moved, the only option is to move the electricity it makes. Sometimes that's a long trip. Wind farms require a lot of space, so they are usually built in distant areas, far from where most people live. Currently, the U.S. and other nations are struggling to build enough transmission lines to carry all that power. If there is no way to deliver the electricity, turbines have to be shut down. That's made some developers wary of building more wind farms.

---

*The Bahrain World Trade Center was the first skyscraper
to incorporate wind turbines into its design.*

Another hurdle is that wind has its own schedule. It blows when it blows. It never considers whether the timing is convenient for humans who would like some electricity to microwave popcorn and watch TV. When there's not enough wind blowing, there must be some kind of backup system in place to provide electricity to customers. Electricity is not impossible to store, but it's expensive. Power plant operators usually decide to "use it or lose it"—but not save it. An ongoing challenge is trying to balance the amount of wind available with the demand for electricity.

One way to take advantage of wind's schedule is to use it in **hybrid** systems. These systems combine wind with another source of energy, such as solar or hydropower. The sun shines only during the day, but wind is stronger at night. Wind also increases during winter, when solar energy is less powerful. If they are used together, they can balance each other out. Hydropower is another good pairing. Hydroelectricity, produced from the force of water rushing downward, can be used during the day, when demand is high. At night, wind power can pump the water back up for its use again the next day.

Wind-generated electricity also works for the electrolysis of water. This is the process of separating water into its two chemical parts, oxygen and hydrogen. The hydrogen is then stored in a fuel cell, where it can be converted into electricity. Creative solutions such as this are helping make wind more attractive in the

Wind and solar power systems work well together because their efficiencies peak at complementary times.

CHAPTER THREE

GETTING ON
THE GRID

WIND ISN'T LIKELY TO SOLVE THE ENERGY ISSUES OF THE FUTURE—NOT BY ITSELF, ANYWAY. But many experts say that's not the point. Instead of relying on one kind of energy, people can mix and match according to what makes sense for their lifestyles and budgets.

In the 1990s and 2000s, governments began to get serious about pursuing renewable energy. Many countries have set goals to increase how much energy they will use from renewable sources. By 2020, wind power in Europe is expected to increase to provide about 12 to 14 percent of the continent's electricity. Denmark alone wants to have half of its electricity generation from wind by then.

With wind as its main energy contributor, Denmark plans to be completely free of fossil fuels by 2050.

Turbines at Burbo Bank Offshore Wind Farm in England's Liverpool Bay are designed to run for 20 years.

Across the ocean, the U.S. government predicts that 20 percent of the country's electricity could come from wind by 2030. Globally, wind power could supply about 9 percent of the world's electric needs by 2020. In 2011, a **tsunami** caused a meltdown at a nuclear power plant in Japan. After the disaster, many countries pledged to phase out nuclear power altogether. The push toward renewable energy became even more urgent.

Growth in wind energy production is expected all over the world, from Eastern Europe and Russia to Canada and Australia. Developing countries in Africa and Asia are also looking to wind. In the past, South America and Latin America have depended heavily on hydropower. When the weather is dry, however, rivers run low and slow, making it difficult to produce enough electricity. On the other hand, wind tends to increase in drier weather, so that energy form could take up the slack.

Another huge market is China. China is the largest country in the world in terms of population, and it's growing all the time. Many of its citizens still do not have access to electricity, but that's changing. As more and more people get on the grid, the Chinese government is targeting wind energy to meet about 8 percent of its electricity demand by 2020. Part of the plan is to build a series of wind farms at several "megabases" throughout the country. These would consist of hundreds of turbines churning out dozens of gigawatts of electricity. The country is also bumping up offshore wind power.

In 2011, U.S. researchers conducted a study to estimate how much global wind energy there really is. Their results indicated that wind could supply at least half the world's total energy needs, and maybe more, by 2030. Doing so would require about 4 million turbines to be installed around the globe. "Four million turbines is a lot, but it's not impossible," said Cristina Archer, a professor at the University of Delaware who worked on the study. "The

benefits are immense—we'd have a clean economy and we'd be getting rid of pollution. If society wants to do it, the technology is there—it's not like we have to invent **cold fusion** from scratch."

At the other end of the spectrum are small wind systems. They produce only a fraction of the amount of electricity of larger plants. But there are many more places they could go. Such systems are ideal for poor or remote areas. People in such places are often not wired to the power grid, and could not afford to purchase its electricity, even if they were connected. But small, local systems can provide enough electricity to power a generator that can run lights or appliances, and many small wind systems have been installed around the globe.

Villages such as Dhule, India, are home to large corporate wind farms.

Implementing renewable energy often means new routines, such as plugging in electric cars overnight.

Wind operates on its own timetable, so another challenge is how to best get on its schedule. In Denmark, officials are looking at putting more electric cars onto the road. They could be plugged into the grid at night—when wind is high—to recharge. Such systems are also in development in Israel and parts of the U.S., including Hawaii and Northern California.

The basic technology of wind power is in place, but there's still room for improvement. Future turbines are being designed to be more efficient, durable, and noninvasive. Some will be quieter. Others will take advantage of lower wind speeds. One idea that's literally up in the air is that of airborne wind turbines. Like giant kites or balloons, these turbines could climb to altitudes of about 1,000 feet (305 m), where they can access stronger winds. Electricity would be sent to the ground via cables. Another technology would use the force of the wind to push a stack of electrodes together. Electrodes are devices that conduct electricity. The pressure would generate an electric current.

A common way to store energy is in batteries. However, batteries are not particularly economical. They make sense for a flashlight in case the power goes out, but they cost a lot for the relatively small amount of energy they store. Also, to stash all the energy produced by wind electricity, a battery would have to be huge! There's progress being made on that front, though. Researchers in the U.S. are

Underwater power cables, or submarine cables, may be as small in diameter as garden hoses.

working on a liquid metal battery they believe will be ideal for storing excess energy from renewable sources such as wind and solar. It holds a lot of energy for its size, lasts a long time, and is relatively inexpensive.

At the Iowa Stored Energy Park in the U.S., engineers are working on another idea. When demand for electricity is low, extra wind power would run an air compressor. It would pump air underground and store it at high pressures. When demand went back up, the air would be released and mixed with natural gas to drive a turbine. Engineers predict such a system would be about 50 percent more efficient than a turbine run just by fossil fuels. The designers noted, "By storing the wind's

energy for when we need it, wind is something we can control and count upon." The facility has a target operational date of 2015.

One statistic says that the wind in North Dakota alone could supply a third of the power needed for the whole U.S. That seems encouraging for wind, but the problem is that not very many people live in North Dakota. Other countries face similar issues. All that electricity must travel from its source to the people who will use it, and sometimes that takes several hundred miles. Wind energy needs a bigger and better **infrastructure** of "transmission corridors," or power lines. These lines are expensive, and it takes a long time to build them.

Jack-up rig platforms are used in constructing offshore wind farms.

Most households use alternating current electricity rather than the direct current variety. However, alternating current loses much of its power when it's moved over long distances. Some future transmission lines may instead use high-voltage direct current (HVDC) to get around this problem. HVDC is like an express train: it's well suited to moving electricity quickly and over long distances, as long as there are no layovers. Some underwater HVDC cables have already been installed to bring power from offshore wind farms in the Atlantic to the highly populated cities on the East Coast, and more such cables are planned. In the Midwest, an HVDC line called the "Grain Belt Express" would take wind energy from Kansas and move it east into Missouri and Illinois.

The term "soft energy" describes energy that is renewable and flexible. It takes advantage of natural conditions and makes it a good energy source for the people who live in those environments. Wind power, solar energy, and certain types of hydropower are all candidates for soft energy. Most people today rely on fossil fuel plants that provide large amounts of power through a sophisticated grid. But the future may bring more energy that is produced at the local level, and in smaller amounts. Fortunately, wind can be downsized in some places, even as larger wind farms do more of the heavy lifting. It comes in small, medium, and large varieties!

CHAPTER FOUR

TILTING AT WINDMILLS

IN AN OLD SPANISH NOVEL, THE HERO, DON QUIXOTE, COMES ACROSS A FIELD FULL OF WINDMILLS. He mistakes them for enemies, and begins to joust, or "tilt," at these imagined foes. Today, the wind industry faces a battle from people who think wind power is too expensive, inefficient, and even dangerous to be used as a significant energy source. On the other side are proponents who argue that wind power—even with its challenges—is a no-brainer.

In the Altamont Pass of Northern California, thousands of wind turbines dot the landscape. Built in the early 1980s, it was one of the first large-scale wind projects in the U.S. Some people thought it was the first step toward a future of clean, renewable energy. However, Altamont Pass had problems. Not only did the turbines not always work reliably, but it turned out the farm was put in an area that is a freeway for **migrating** birds. When endangered bird species began to be killed by the spinning blades of turbines, environmentalists protested. Bird deaths are a problem not only at Altamont Pass but also at wind farms across the world.

It's impossible to know just how many birds are killed by turbines, but estimates range from about 50,000 to 200,000 per year. The turbines are also a problem for bats. Sometimes they collide with the blades or are killed when their lungs **hemorrhage**. Their bodies cannot handle the dramatic changes in air pressure found near the rotating blades. In addition to

In 2013, Toronto protesters dressed as eagles, which are often displaced or killed by wind turbines.

direct deaths, wind farms can be disruptive to the habitats of native wildlife. This makes wind energy especially controversial in places that are home to a large variety of species. Wind developers often study the possible environmental effects before erecting a wind farm, but some people aren't sure that's enough. Angelo Capparella, an **ornithologist** and evolutionary biology professor in Illinois, has closely followed the progress of wind farms in his area. After reviewing the environmental impact reports submitted by developers, he's concerned that the studies aren't telling the whole story. He says, "It is clear, to me at least, the farms are going up faster than the science [is progressing]."

However, improvements to wind farms are being made. At Altamont Pass, the problems were partly because the industry was so new, and people were still learning how wind

turbines affected wildlife and the environment in the 1990s. At Altamont, for example, the turbines spun very quickly, increasing bird deaths. Today's turbines are much slower, and taller, out of the paths of birds. Some wind companies have installed sophisticated radar systems that can detect incoming birds and shut down the turbines until the birds have passed. The St. Nikola Kavarna wind farm in the southeastern European country of Bulgaria is situated on a popular bird freeway. There, an ornithologist is on-site to keep watch during busy migration periods. In 2010, strong winds blew some 30,000 migrating storks off course. The resident ornithologist put out a "stop" order. Within five seconds, the turbines stopped spinning, and the birds passed safely.

New U.S. wind farms must be in bird-friendly locations.

People can also be negatively affected by wind turbines. Most people who oppose wind farms simply don't like looking at them. They say the turbines ruin the view, and they're worried the machines will bring down the value of their property. However, some people complain that the noise and movement of turbines makes them physically sick. Wind turbines seem quiet, but they do produce **low-frequency noise**. This causes tinnitus (ringing of the ears) in some people. Other people have experienced nausea, blurry vision, headaches, and sleeplessness. Doctors have named this collection of symptoms "wind turbine syndrome." No studies prove that wind turbines can cause health problems, but there is a lot of **anecdotal** evidence. Another problem is "shadow flicker" caused when the sun moves behind the rotating turbines. The pulsating light can be annoying, and some people complain it causes headaches and dizziness. Some residents who live near turbines have had to put blackout curtains, which block out all light, on their windows to keep the flickering out of their living rooms!

Traditionally, larger wind turbines have been situated outside city limits or in less-populated areas.

Constant energy production requires not only wind power but also fossil fuels such as coal.

Meanwhile, there are objections that wind energy alone isn't going to save the planet. Wind may not create greenhouse gases, but it will not get rid of them, either. That's because wind blows only some of the time. To produce electricity during down times, fossil fuel plants must ramp up to fill the void. Producing surges of power takes more energy than it does to keep a plant running at a constant pace. As a result, more carbon dioxide and other greenhouse gases and pollutants are released. Proponents of wind energy, however, argue that the amount is relatively small, compared with how clean wind is overall. There's another side to this question: Will global warming affect the amount of wind? Some scientists think that global warming will make wind weaker because of a smaller difference in the temperature between warm and cool air. Others think just the opposite. One study showed that, over a 30-year period leading up to 2008, worldwide wind speeds decreased. However, that data was mostly collected at heights of 33 feet (10 m), whereas wind turbines are much higher up.

Noise, the view, global warming, cost—there are plenty of objections to wind. And there have been some hiccups in wind development, too. In 2008, developers announced plans for a South Dakota wind farm that would be the largest in the world. As of 2013, those plans had not been put into effect, though. In England, several projects lost support and were abandoned. But for the most part, governments are deciding that the benefits of wind outweigh the drawbacks.

The world has yet to harness the full potential of wind power.

One potential benefit of wind is its ability to provide "energy security." The more that countries can supply their own energy, the less they rely on importing it from other nations. Turning to **domestic** sources gives countries a measure of independence because it frees them up from having to negotiate with other countries to buy fuel. Buying within their borders means that the prices are more stable, and there is less risk of the supply being cut off altogether. Shorter transport distances can also bring the price down.

In many countries, the wind industry has been helped by a financial incentive called a feed-in tariff (FIT). This guarantees that producers will have a market for the wind energy they produce and that they will be paid a certain amount of money for the power they "feed in" to the electric grid. Wind farms are more expensive to build than fossil fuel plants, but the upside is that they have relatively short payback times. It takes less than a year for a wind plant to produce more energy than it took to build the farm. Meanwhile, prices for turbines are coming down, making projects cheaper to pursue. In some of the most productive areas for wind power, such as Montana, the price of wind energy is already competitive with fossil fuels. Experts say that the global industry as a whole will be able to compete by 2020.

Wind could also benefit from a new way of distributing electricity. A "smart grid" could automatically dispense electricity during times of low demand for tasks that are not as time-sensitive as others (such as running the dishwasher). In addition, if a small-scale wind system used by an individual or community makes extra electricity, it could be sold back to the grid for someone else to use. It would be the ultimate "extra credit"!

Most nations today are working to make renewable energy a bigger part of their energy mix—and the faster, the better. As the wind industry has developed over the last few decades, it's become clearer just how valuable a resource it can be. It has also made its drawbacks more apparent. The future of wind energy will likely depend on finding the right path for it. Just as air will seep through the cracks around a drafty window, wind power may soon fill the cracks of how people use energy.

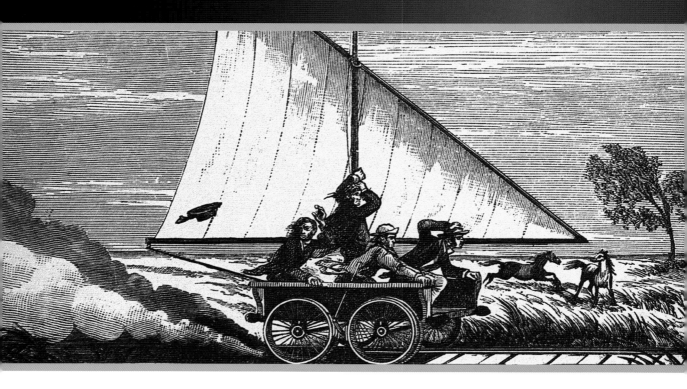

In the 1180s, a European farmer named Herbert built a windmill. This enterprising act enraged a local church official. He had a watermill and wanted the locals—including Herbert—to pay him to use it. Herbert argued that "the free benefit of the wind ought not to be denied to any man." The clergyman was unimpressed. Even if he did not own the wind, he stated that he controlled what buildings or structures could be built in the area. Herbert's windmill, the official determined, was against the law. Before Herbert could object any more and get into trouble, his sons took it down for him.

Horses and wagons were the most common way to travel across the American West in the 1800s, but some ingenious settlers found another way. They used "wind wagons," which had wheels on the bottom and a sail on top. In 1860, a man named Samuel Peppard built a wind wagon to sail from Kansas City to Denver. His neighbors laughed, calling the idea "Peppard's Folly," but he proved them wrong. The wagon traveled about 15 miles (24 km) per hour and occasionally as fast as 40 miles (64 km) per hour. Peppard covered about 500 miles (800 km) before the wagon was blown to pieces by the constant wind.

Before the well-known expedition of Peppard's Folly, other Kansas residents employed the prairie's natural resource for their own wind or "sailing" wagons (above).

Some people build a tennis court or swimming pool in their backyard, but Charles Brush had something else in mind. In 1888, the Cleveland, Ohio, electrical engineer and inventor built the first wind turbine designed to generate electricity on a large scale. It was 60 feet (18 m) tall and weighed 80,000 pounds (36,300 kg). The giant windmill powered a "dynamo," or electrical generator, that fed power to batteries that Brush installed in his basement. The machine generated enough electricity to power 350 lights and a variety of small machines. The machine operated until Brush dismantled it in 1908.

When he wasn't teaching math or physics, the Danish inventor Poul La Cour was figuring out how to keep the lights on at his high school. In 1891, La Cour began experimenting with using wind energy to create electricity, which was then used in the electrolysis of water—the separation of water into hydrogen and oxygen. La Cour then stored the hydrogen and used it to power the gaslights at his school. La Cour resumed studying the mechanics of wind later in the 1890s. He determined that windmills worked best when they had fewer blades and turned faster. His discoveries in **aerodynamics** are still at work in the construction of wind turbines today.

Charles Brush's (left) Brush Electric Company later merged to become General Electric. In the 1300s, European tower mills (right) were the most efficient windmills to that point.

Georges Jean Marie Darrieus decided to turn things around. In 1931, the French aeronautical engineer patented a wind turbine that rotated on a vertical **axis**. Instead of propellers on sticks, his design resembled an eggbeater, or a whisk, with curved blades bowing out from a central shaft. One advantage of vertical-axis turbines is that they can adapt more easily to the direction the wind is blowing. However, they sit close to the ground, where they can't reach stronger winds at higher altitudes. This makes them less efficient, and they are not widely used today.

The world was searching for alternative energy sources after the oil crisis in 1973. By 1980, American company US Windpower had constructed the world's first wind farm on Crotched Mountain in New Hampshire. It was a modest attempt by today's standards. There were only 20 turbines, and they provided just 30 kilowatts of power each. The Crotched wind farm failed. The turbines broke and US Windpower lost a lot of money. However, it learned from its mistakes and went on to build several more wind farms in California, helping to launch the modern wind industry in the U.S.

Newer models of vertical-axis turbines (left) are designed for use in crowded urban areas, but horizontal-axis turbines (center) have proven to be more efficient and reliable.

The wind farm in Vindeby, Denmark, was groundbreaking—in a way. When it was installed, it didn't "break ground," since it was built in the ocean off the country's coast. But that's exactly what made it a pioneering project in wind energy development. With 11 turbines, it was the world's first commercial offshore wind farm. The project was conceived as an experiment to study offshore wind patterns and plan the development of future offshore wind farms. The first electricity was piped onshore in the summer of 1991. More than 20 years later, the Vindeby wind farm was still going strong, powering more than 2,700 homes each year.

It's not recommended to fly a jumbo jet through the sweep of the world's largest wind turbine, but it's possible. With blades that are 246 feet (75 m) long, these turbines cover an area of 200,000 square feet (18,600 sq m) in a rotation. The blade tips travel at 180 miles (290 km) per hour. The fiberglass blades are only one piece, cast in a giant mold. They're so big they wouldn't even fit inside a warehouse to be painted. Instead, workers had to paint them on-site. The turbines began testing in 2012 for an offshore wind farm in Denmark.

Researchers perform large-scale tests on rotor blades (right) and other wind turbine designs and materials to develop better safety, longevity, and efficiency in the industry.

GLOSSARY

aerodynamics—the study of air movement and how it interacts with objects

anecdotal—unofficial, informal

anemometer—a device that measures wind speed

axis—a central line around which something revolves

cold fusion—an unproven, and perhaps impossible, technology to produce a nuclear reaction

corrode—to eat away, gradually damage

domestic—within any given nation; not involving other countries

fossil fuels—fuels formed by decaying plants and animals over millions of years

global warming—the phenomenon of Earth's average temperatures increasing over time

greenhouse gas—a gas that builds up in Earth's atmosphere and prevents the release of heat

hemorrhage—to bleed uncontrollably

hybrid—a combination of two or more things, used to complement one another

Industrial Revolution—a period from the late 1700s through the 1800s in Europe and the U.S. marked by a shift from economies based on agriculture and handicraft to ones dominated by mechanized production in factories

infrastructure—the services and mechanisms used to support a society

low-frequency noise—sound that is below the limit of normal human hearing but can affect the body through vibration

medieval—relating to a time in Europe from about the fifth century A.D. to 1453

migrating—traveling over a long distance in a regular pattern

ornithologist—a person who studies birds

pollinated—fertilized for growth

power grid—a system for distributing power throughout a community

renewable—able to be replenished and used indefinitely

topography—the characteristics of a landscape

tsunami—a large ocean wave triggered by an earthquake

turbine—a machine that is driven by water, steam, or a gas flowing through the blades of a wheel

SELECTED BIBLIOGRAPHY

Behr, Peter. "Fickle Winds, Intermittent Sunshine Start to Stress U.S. Power System." NYTimes.com. April 25, 2011. http://www.nytimes.com/cwire/2011/04/25/25climatewire-fickle-winds-intermittent-sunshine-start-to-52967.html?pagewanted=all.

Busby, Rebecca. *Wind Power: The Industry Grows Up.* Tulsa, Okla.: PennWell Corporation, 2012.

Chiras, Dan. *Wind Power Basics.* Gabriola Island, B.C.: New Society Publishers, 2010.

Lynn, Paul A. *Onshore and Offshore Wind Energy.* Hoboken, N.J.: Wiley, 2012.

Markham, Derek. "The Future of Wind Power: 9 Cool Innovations." TreeHugger.com. April 4, 2012. http://www.treehugger.com/wind-technology/future-wind-power-9-cool-innovations.html.

Musgrove, Peter. *Wind Power.* Cambridge: Cambridge University Press, 2010.

Righter, Robert. *Windfall: Wind Energy in America Today.* Norman: University of Oklahoma Press, 2011.

Roney, J. Matthew. "World Wind Power Climbs to New Record in 2011." Earth Policy Institute. March 14, 2012. http://www.earth-policy.org/indicators/C49/wind_power_2012.

Shepherd, William, and Li Zhang. *Electricity Generation Using Wind Power.* Singapore: World Scientific Publishing, 2011.

Kids Ahead

http://kidsahead.com/subjects/2-wind-energy/activities
This website offers links to a variety of activities that demonstrate wind power in action and to sites that explore how wind energy works.

U.S. Energy Information Administration

http://www.eia.gov/kids/energy.cfm?page=wind_home-basics
This section of the U.S. Energy Information Administration's website provides information on wind power's history, how it works, and where it's used.

NOTE: *Every effort has been made to ensure that the websites listed above are suitable for children, that they have educational value, and that they contain no inappropriate material. However, because of the nature of the Internet, it is impossible to guarantee that these sites will remain active indefinitely or that their contents will not be altered.*

Dorion, Christiane. *Are We Running out of Energy?* Mankato, Minn.: Arcturus, 2008.

Gunderson, Jessica. *The Energy Dilemma*. Mankato, Minn.: Creative Education, 2011.

Morris, Neil. *The Energy Mix*. Mankato, Minn.: Smart Apple Media, 2010.

————. *Wind Power*. Mankato, Minn.: Smart Apple Media, 2010.

Oxlade, Chris. *Energy Technology*. Mankato, Minn.: Smart Apple Media, 2012.

Royston, Angela. *Sustainable Energy*. Mankato, Minn.: Arcturus, 2009.

Solway, Andrew. *Climate Change*. Mankato, Minn.: Smart Apple Media, 2010.

HARNESSING ENERGY · HARNESSING ENERGY

Published by Creative Paperbacks
P.O. Box 227, Mankato, Minnesota 56002
Creative Paperbacks is an imprint of The Creative Company
www.thecreativecompany.us

Design and production by The Design Lab
Art direction by Rita Marshall
Printed in the United States of America

Photographs by Alamy (Ashley Cooper pics, Image Asset Management Ltd., Alex
Segre), Corbis (Bettmann, Amit Bhargava, Ashley Cooper, Francis Cormon/Hemis,
PAWEL KOPCZYNSKI/Reuters, Ocean, Jochen Tack/imagebroker, Ingo Wagner/
dpa), Dreamstime (Wessel Cirkel, Euclem, Micka, Marcin Okupniak, Tupungato,
Aleksandr Ugorenkov), Shutterstock (anweber, Sissy Borbely, Orhan Cam, David Carillet,
IgorGolovniov, Jesus Keller, igor kisselev, Przemek Klos, kwest, J. Marijs, msgrafixx, Alta
Oosthuizen, pedrosala, Nicram Sabod, sunsinger, Eugene Suslo, Vlue, WDG Photo)

Library of Congress Cataloging-in-Publication Data
Bailey, Diane.
Wind power / Diane Bailey.
p. cm. — (Harnessing energy)
Includes bibliographical references and index.
Summary: An examination of the ways in which wind has historically been
used as an energy source and how current and future energy demands
are changing its technical applications and efficiency levels.
ISBN 978-1-60818-413-2 (hardcover)
ISBN 978-0-89812-999-1 (pbk)
1. Wind power—Juvenile literature. 2. Wind power plants—Juvenile literature. I. Title.

TJ820.B347 2014
621.31'2136—dc23   2013035757

CCSS: RI.5.1, 2, 3, 4, 8, 9

First Edition
9 8 7 6 5 4 3 2 1